Aitziber Lopez - Luciano Lozano

BRILLIANT IDEAS
FROM WONDERFUL WOMEN

WIDE EYED EDITIONS

THE
CAR
HEATER
1893

Margaret A. Wilcox

Born in Chicago in 1838, Margaret was one of the few female mechanical engineers of her time. She loved coming up with inventions that anyone could use that would improve people's lives.

At the time, cars had no heating system. People would shiver and freeze during the long hours they spent behind the wheel. Can you imagine driving around in the middle of winter with snow all around you and nothing to keep you warm? Brrr!

Margaret wanted to put an end to the cold conditions drivers had to endure. So, in 1893, when Margaret was 34, she devised a mechanism that directed the waste hot air from the vehicle's engine to the driver's seat, keeping them nice and warm.

People loved her new invention, but it became a health and safety risk because there was no way of controlling how high the temperature got. As a result, her design could not be used. However, it is the inspiration behind the car heating systems used today.

Margaret is also credited with the invention of the first washing machine.

MONOPOLY,
A GAME FOR
EVERYONE
1904

Elizabeth Magie Phillips

Born in 1866 in Illinois, USA, Elizabeth Magie Phillips was an entrepreneur and toy designer. Her family fought against slavery, and Elizabeth was very young when she had to drop out of school so she could help support her family financially. She worked as a stenographer, a writer, a journalist, an actress, and a comedian.

At the time, there were no televisions, computers, or video games and even books were scarce in most households because they were so expensive. People found other ways to entertain themselves, and often played board games and cards.

Elizabeth invented a game called The Landlord's Game, which would go on to inspire the famous board game Monopoly. Elizabeth designed the game around her political beliefs; she wanted people to see that monopolizing lands and resources was a bad idea since it meant some people got richer and richer while others became poorer and poorer.

Elizabeth was never properly credited during her lifetime for the role she played in the creation of Monopoly. It wasn't until 40 years after her death that it was uncovered that Elizabeth came up with the idea for the most famous board game of all time.

DISPOSABLE DIAPERS
1951

Marion O'Brien Donovan

Marion O'Brien Donovan was born in 1917 in Indiana, USA, to a family of inventors. She studied English literature and worked as an editorial assistant at various fashion magazines.

When Marion's first daughter was born, diapers were made out of cloth, which meant they had to be washed by hand so they could be used again. And unlike diapers today, they weren't waterproof, so often leaked onto bedsheets! The poor babies were constantly wet and their mothers ended up with very sore hands from so much cleaning and scrubbing. What a nightmare!

Marion was tired of washing and rewashing the cloth diapers and bedsheets, and it wasn't long before the inventor's blood running through her veins kicked into action. Marion designed a waterproof diaper cover using the same material that parachutes are made from.

Marion went on to invent many other things, including dental floss, a hanger that could hold 30 garments, and a soap dish that drained into the sink.

Marion wanted to take her invention a step further and went on to develop a disposable diaper made from nylon that was sold all over the world! Although the idea was not very environmentally friendly, mothers rejoiced at the new product. They no longer had to do mounds of laundry, and babies were free from diaper rash and constantly being wet.

THE **DISHWASHER**
1886

Josephine Garis Cochrane

Josephine Garis Cochrane was born in 1839 in Ohio, USA, to a wealthy family. As a child, Josephine would sometimes go with her father, a civil engineer, to work—perhaps inspiring her love of mechanics at a young age!

Like many wealthy women of her time, once Josephine was married, she gave up her studies and devoted herself to family life and to running the household. She organized many events including cocktail and dinner parties, which always resulted in mounds of dirty plates—all of which had to be washed by hand at the end of the night!

Josephine wondered why nobody had invented a machine to do the job and so she came up with a design herself. Her idea was a copper boiler with a wheel in it. The dirty dishes and glasses were placed on a type of shelf and jets of hot water sprayed through the wheel at them. And it worked!

After Josephine's husband died, she became an inventor. Her dishwasher invention was not the first, but she was the first to have the idea of marketing her invention to every home, restaurant, and hotel that needed it.

DOMESTIC SURVEILLANCE SYSTEM
1966

Marie Van Brittan Brown

Born in 1922, Marie was an African American nurse and inventor. She lived all her life in the Queens borough of New York City, with her husband, Albert Brown, an electronic technician.

In the late 1960s, Queens could be a dangerous neighborhood. High crime rates coupled with the fact that the police could not always arrive on time when needed meant that people in the area often felt unsafe in their own homes. Marie and Albert worked different hours than each other, which meant that Marie was often left alone at home. To feel safer when home alone, Marie and her husband devised a system to identify anyone who knocked on their front door.

At the time, patenting and marketing an invention as a woman was not easy, but it was even more difficult trying to do this as a black woman. Sadly, Marie and her husband were unsuccessful in marketing their surveillance system, but many others made their fortune later, inspired by their patent.

The invention was a set of four peepholes, a camera, and a microphone, all of which were placed in the main door of the house. The camera could move up and down and look out through each peephole and anything the camera picked up was then fed back onto a television monitor, allowing Brown to see who was outside her house without ever opening the door. The system also included two buttons: one opened the door to allow the person outside in and the other triggered an alarm to alert neighbors that you were in danger.

KEVLAR®
1965

Stephanie Kwolek

Stephanie Kwolek was a chemist born in Pennsylvania, USA, in 1923 to a family of Polish immigrants.

Stephanie researched compounds called polymers, which are long chains of small molecules called monomers. These molecules can be natural, such as silk, or synthetic, such as polyethylene.

In 1965, Stephanie created an opaque, liquid substance. Everyone thought she had made a mistake—up until that point any substances that had been created had been either transparent or viscous. Nobody had seen anything like it before! But Stephanie didn't give up on her discovery and continued researching and working on her new material until that substance was converted into a super-resistant, flexible, and lightweight fiber with hundreds of uses. They named it the Kevlar® fiber.

Kevlar® is a material as strong as steel and as light as a feather. It is used to make tennis rackets, skis, rope, fireman helmets, satellites, tires, space rockets, bulletproof vests, and lots of other things. The discovery of this material didn't only improve lives—it saved them!

SEA FLARES
1859

Martha Coston

Martha Coston was born in 1826 in Baltimore, USA. When she was about 16 years old, she ran away from home and secretly married Benjamin Franklin Coston, a promising inventor. Their love story was like something from the movies!

Benjamin was actually the one who had the initial idea for the sea flares. However, before he could develop the idea, he died. Martha was left a widow at just 21 years old, with three small children to look after, but thanks to her perseverance, she managed to develop and patent the invention.

In order to develop Benjamin's designs for the sea flare, Martha disguised herself as a man. This enabled her to contact pyrotechnicians and convince them to manufacture her idea. They would never have taken her seriously if they'd known she was a woman.

Radios did not exist at the time and so sea flares were vital for sea captains and sailors. They were used as a means of communication between ships, especially at night. The code they used was based on three colors: white, red, and green—a language that all sailors knew. They are still the most useful way to locate boats at sea today.

NON REFLECTIVE GLASS
1940

Katharine Burr Blodgett

Born in New York, USA, in 1898, Katharine Burr was the first woman to get a PhD in physics at the University of Cambridge.

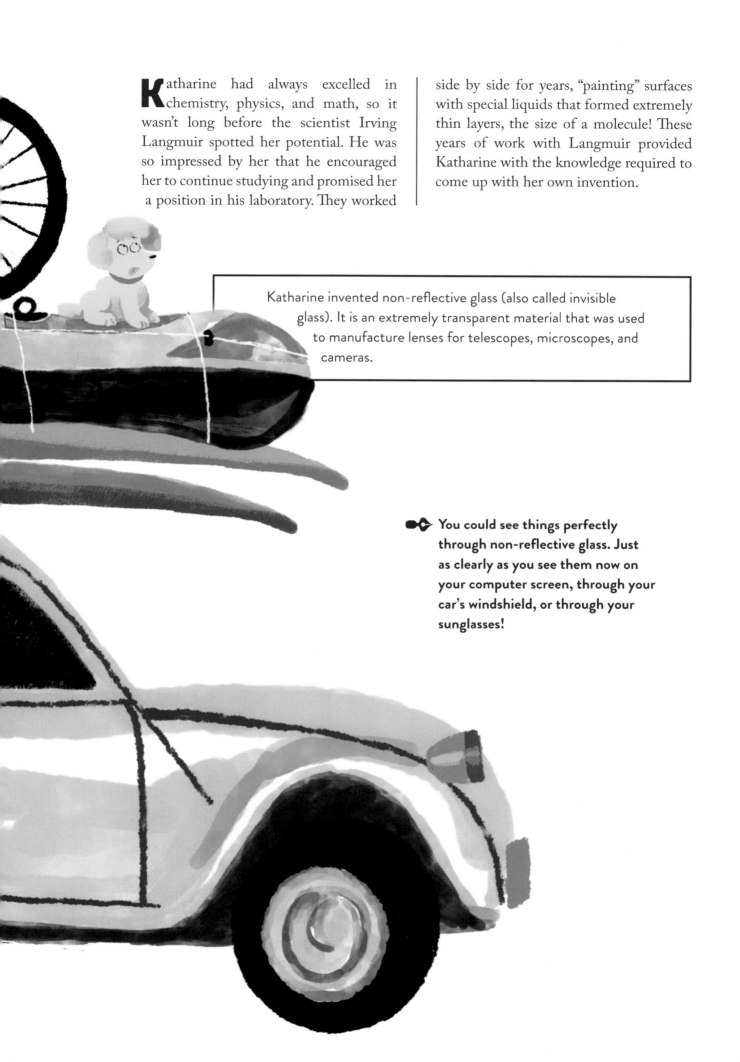

Katharine had always excelled in chemistry, physics, and math, so it wasn't long before the scientist Irving Langmuir spotted her potential. He was so impressed by her that he encouraged her to continue studying and promised her a position in his laboratory. They worked side by side for years, "painting" surfaces with special liquids that formed extremely thin layers, the size of a molecule! These years of work with Langmuir provided Katharine with the knowledge required to come up with her own invention.

Katharine invented non-reflective glass (also called invisible glass). It is an extremely transparent material that was used to manufacture lenses for telescopes, microscopes, and cameras.

You could see things perfectly through non-reflective glass. Just as clearly as you see them now on your computer screen, through your car's windshield, or through your sunglasses!

THE
FIRST WI-FI,
BLUETOOTH, AND GPS
1942

Hedy Lamarr

Hedy Lamarr was born in Vienna, Austria, in 1914, to a Jewish family. Her real name was Hedwig Eva Maria Kiesler, and as well as being an inventor and engineer, Hedy was also a huge Hollywood star.

During World War II, the famous Hollywood star Hedy Lamarr and the American composer and artist George Antheil invented a secret communication system together. It was a form of long-distance wireless communication that was used to detect torpedoes. Perhaps one of the most curious things about this invention was that it was inspired by piano keys!

Years later, Hedy's idea went on to become the basis for the design of Wi-Fi.

The aim of their secret communication system was to help with the fight against the Nazis. Years before inventing it, Hedy was forced to marry a businessman and arms merchant named Friedrich Mandl. He kept Hedy locked up at home and only let her out to attend social events or meetings with senior Nazi officials. At these meetings, she overheard many secrets about the Nazi military—information that she would later put to good use while working on her invention.

THE
MEDICAL
SYRINGE
1899

Letitia Mumford Geer

Letitia was a New York nurse born in 1852 who invented the first glass syringe. It contained glass parts and could be used with just one hand.

You might think this doesn't sound like much, but before her invention, syringes were made of metal and were very difficult to use. You needed two hands to hold the syringe, and in most cases, you had to rely on the help of an assistant to administer it.

The one-hand operated syringe was a medical breakthrough! It allowed doctors and nurses to use their free hand for other tasks, meaning that they could better treat their patient. Nowadays, health professionals use syringes that are single-use and even simpler to use.

Letitia patented her invention in 1899. She used her imagination to invent an object that not only made many people's jobs easier, but that went on to improve the health and lives of many people.

THE SUBMARINE TELESCOPE 1845

Sarah Mather

Little is known about Sarah Mather. However, we do know that in 1845 she patented an incredible idea: the submarine telescope.

The patented design of the submarine telescope was very simple. It was a tube with a lamp on it making it possible to see under the water. The invention could be used to examine the hulls of boats, discover objects underwater, study the seabed, or go fishing.

Over the years, and thanks to technological improvements, the submarine telescope has evolved to become the instrument we know today. It is an essential tool in all submarines, especially research ones, which analyze the seabed and discover underwater mountains, valleys, and new marine species.

Quite often there are no records of female inventors' births, who their relatives were, or where they lived. Sometimes we can't even find a photograph of them. But we do have something that survives the passing of time: their inventions.

Helen is one of the world's foremost experts in diagnostic systems. She is now retired, although continues working to promote scientific education in society, especially among women and the less-advantaged.

DIAGNOSTIC TESTS
1959

Helen Murray Free

Born in Pennsylvania, USA, in 1923, Helen initially wanted to study English and Latin. However, she ended up specializing in chemistry and, as soon as she finished her degree, started working in a laboratory as a researcher.

Together with her husband, Helen created the first diagnostic tests for different diseases (such as diabetes). Diagnostic tests are quick ways for doctors to find out if a patient is sick.

Helen's new "dip-and-read" test meant that, instead of doing a blood test, doctors could use strips of paper that changed color when placed in urine to indicate whether a patient had diabetes.

THE LIFE RAFT
1882

Maria Beasley

Born in Philadelphia, USA, in 1847, Maria Beasley was a great businesswoman, inventor, and entrepreneur who had several jobs before one of her inventions really took off.

Maria enjoyed improving inventions that already existed. One of her inventions was a life raft that could be launched much more easily and quickly than previous versions. Her improved design meant that the raft worked any way up. So even if it fell into the water upside down, it would still float and support passengers. It also included watertight pockets for storing provisions—a major advance!

The life raft was marketed and sold at a time when it was a common occurrence for boats to sink, often with high death rates. This was due to the fact that there was no sea rescue and many people didn't know how to swim.

Maria's invention was not taken seriously until the sinking of the *Titanic*, one of the biggest maritime disasters of the 20th century. Maria's life rafts were on the ocean liner, but unfortunately there were not enough, and so over 1,000 passengers lost their lives.

THE
WINDSHIELD WIPER
1903

Mary Anderson

Born in 1866 in Alabama, USA, Mary Anderson was a businesswoman and inventor.

On a cold and wet winter's day, Mary Anderson was traveling on a New York tram. It was pouring rain outside, the journey was uncomfortable, and it seemed to last forever. In order to be able to drive safely, the driver had to keep stopping and getting out to clean the rain and snow from the windshield. The experience inspired Mary to develop the first windshield wiper!

The biggest challenge Mary faced wasn't building her invention, but registering it. At the time, a woman needed a man, for example her father, husband, or brother, to register their creations for them. But Mary did not give up and, even though it took her more than two years, she was finally able to register the idea in her own name.

The first windshield wiper was a rubber sheet attached to a spring-loaded metal arm, which was attached to a lever inside the vehicle. The driver could simply pull the lever to clean the glass without having to get out every time to clean the windshield.

THE FIRST E-BOOK
1949

Ángela Ruiz Robles

Ángela was an enthusiastic and innovative inventor born in Villamanín, Spain, in 1895. She trained as a teacher and taught for many years before becoming a headteacher of several schools and institutes. She was also a writer.

Ángela created something very similar to what we now know as the e-book. It was called the "mechanical encyclopedia." The invention contained multiple reels of different books that could be interchanged depending on what you wanted to read. It even had a light for reading in the dark and the potential to play audio!

This modern invention, which allowed teachers to add their own materials and whose portable format meant students would be able to take it to school with them, was way ahead of its time. However, no one invested in it, and so it was forgotten about.

Years later, others would use her idea as the basis for the design of the electronic books (e-books) we use today.

My name is **AITZIBER LOPEZ**. I was born in Aramaio, Álava, Spain, on April 20, 1981, although I moved to Arrasate, Guipúzcoa, when I was two years old. Ever since I was a child, I have been curious and I always knew I wanted to be a scientist. I graduated with a degree in chemistry at the age of 23 and went on to complete a PhD. I have tried to dedicate my career to research, and so far I have been lucky: I worked in a cosmetics company as a product developer, and now I am investigating the world of biomaterials. I love learning something new every day.

LUCIANO LOZANO was born in the same year that man walked on the moon— maybe that's why he traveled a lot from a young age. Self-taught, in 2007, he completed a postgraduate course in creative illustration at the Eina School in Barcelona and has been working as an illustrator since then. He regularly collaborates with numerous publishers and magazines, has received awards for his work, and is nationally and internationally renowned.

His illustrations are characterized by strong colors and textures, as well as by the frequent use of traditional techniques and humor. He currently lives in Barcelona.

www.ilustrista.com

Quarto Knows

Inspiring | Educating | Creating | Entertaining

Brimming with creative inspiration, how-to projects, and useful information to enrich your everyday life, Quarto Knows is a favorite destination for those pursuing their interests and passions. Visit our site and dig deeper with our books into your area of interest: Quarto Creates, Quarto Cooks, Quarto Homes, Quarto Lives, Quarto Drives, Quarto Explores, Quarto Gifts, or Quarto Kids.

Brilliant Ideas From Wonderful Women © 2019 Quarto Publishing plc. Text © 2017 Aitziber Lopez. Illustrations © 2018 Luciano Lozano.

First Published in 2019 by Wide Eyed Editions, an imprint of The Quarto Group. 400 First Avenue North, Suite 400, Minneapolis, MN 55401, USA. T (612) 344-8100 F (612) 344-8692 **www.QuartoKnows.com**

First Published in Spain in 2018 under the title Inventoras Y Sus Inventos by Flamboyant Editorial Flamboyant Bailen, 180 Ground floor, Local 2 08037 Barcelona www.editorialflamboyant.com

The right of Luciano Lozano to be identified as the illustrator and Aitziber Lopez to be identified as the author of this work has been asserted by them in accordance with the Copyright, Designs and Patents Act, 1988 (United Kingdom).

A catalogue record for this book is available from the British Library.

ISBN 978-1-78603-705-3

The illustrations were created digitally • Set in Adobe Caslon Pro, Brandon Grotesque, Overlock, and Intro Cond

Published by Rachel Williams • Designed by Karissa Santos • Edited by Claire Grace Production by Kate O'Riordan and Jenny Cundill

Manufactured in Gunagdong, China TT032019

9 8 7 6 5 4 3 2

FSC
www.fsc.org

MIX
Paper from responsible sources
FSC® C016973

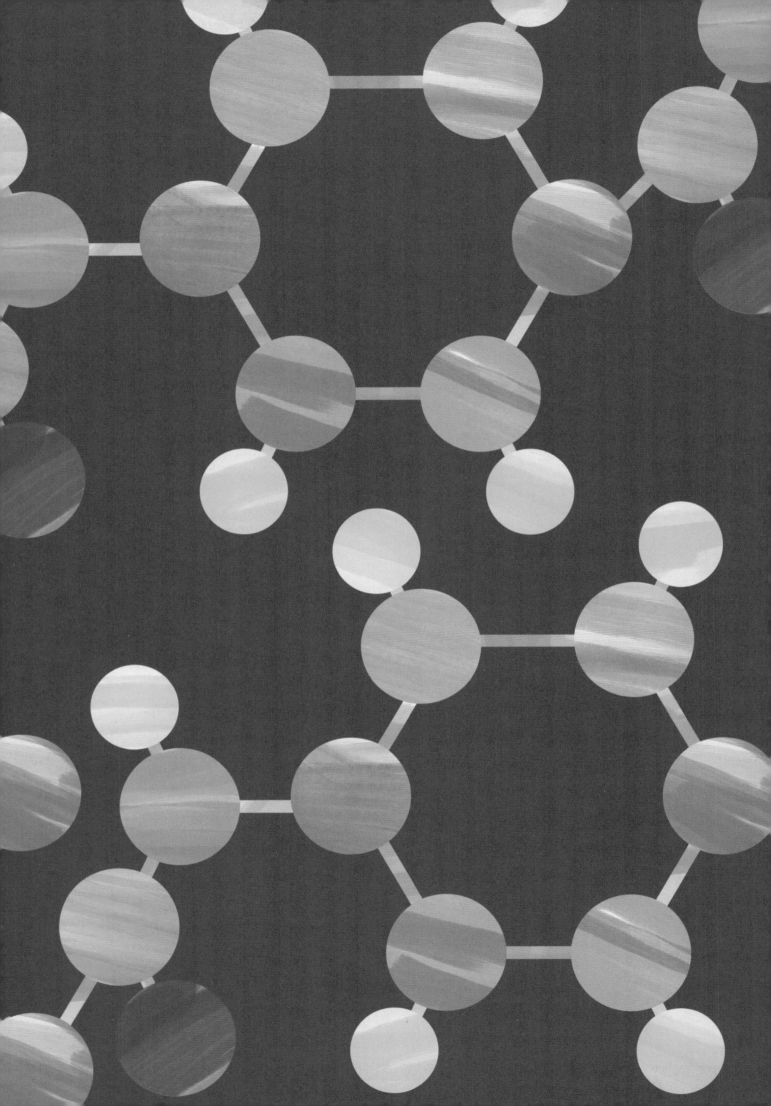